Let it go

Raveena Rawat

BookLeaf Publishing

Presentation by *BookLeaf Publishing*

Web: www.bookleafpub.com

E-mail: info@bookleafpub.com

ISBN:9789358732436

First edition 2023

ACKNOWLEDGEMENT

I would like to thank BookLeaf Publishing for organizing such a remarkable challenge, providing a platform for aspiring writers who love to write and dream of someday publishing their work. Additionally, I am grateful to All poetry websites that have generously offered opportunities to write without charge, allowing me to receive constructive feedback and enhance my skills.

Life

What's Life?
Figuring it out,
answers are in it,
after some time,
hard and easy,
slow and whine,
beautiful memories,
are its divine,
keep going,
not race, on a line.
This is a journey,
all have to find.

~ravenraw

Felt Like Love

Once a guy with black shiny eyes and dark hair,
Moderately tall, broad smile with yellow teeth,
and light skin,
Made me feel like falling for him,
I look and stare from distance,
how his laughs and body waves,
the moment he turned I hide,
Like a child with innocence inside.

~ravenraw

Don't make them Cry

Don't make them cry, who loves you.
Don't make them cry, who cares about you.
Don't make them cry, who do things for you.
You are gonna regret, when they will be no
longer.

I repeat!!
Don't make them cry, who cooks for you.
Don't make them cry, who looks for you.
Don't make them cry, who sings you Lullaby.
You are gonna feel bad, but not surrender.

Don't make them cry, who fights for you.
Don't make them cry, who stays with you.
Don't make them cry, who laughs with you.
You will realize it very later, they will be gone
forever.

So go and ask for forgiveness and apologies,
You got this moment now and never,
It will be too late for your tears to come down,
Fill you with all guilt and sorrows,
So go now And Say You love them,

This is the moment and it will not last forever.

~ravenraw

Diplomat

5

I like morning chorus and peacefulness,
Everyone doing their own thing, yet there is a
silence,
Anything can happen today, as it is a new day.
But I like night too,
when things change,
people are inside their houses,
and speak in a low sense,
I like the silence of it, where my focus is more.
May be it is not morning and night,
but the kind of peace both give me which I like.

~ravenraw

City Girl

Oh! City you have taught me so much.
When I came I only had rawness and innocence.
Now I look back and I see my Past self fade.
Oh! City you have taught me so well.
All these years I look at you with amaze.
Now I see myself as one of your mates.
Oh! City you have taught me so much.
You have so many people and lights.
But my Village had more space and time.
You have so many buildings and Tires,
But my village had many Fires.
When I look back I see a Saayar (Poet),
Who never knew what it takes to be a lawyer.
Oh! City you have given me so much.
And I think I am in Love.
Now I know more and have much desire.
You Gloom everyday that is my Prayer,
I can't thank you enough.
You Will always be my Dear,
Oh! City you have taught me so Much.

~ravenraw

Stay Young

In the time ahead of us, when we will look back,
What are we gonna miss?
Being young, its color, our skin,
Those laughs and stupid things we did.
Clothes we wore and fashion of our prime,
Going in a direction we had no idea about,
Scent of the time, feeling of old wine,
Our stupid decisions and whining in the night,
We are gonna miss,
All the times we took for granted,
Friends we used to share things and our crimes,
We will think to make it better but even,
If given a chance we are gonna repeat the same
again.
Let that be and stay young once again.

~ravenraw

What If I Die Today?

What If I die today? Uncertainly.
All my worries would die with me,
No one will ever know what all they were,
They would go with me forever.
What If I die today? Accidentally
By someone so rude, mean,
All my Sorrow would go away,
In a hope I will be free from them.
And I would take a long breath,
That all my duties end now,
That all my problems end here,
What If I die today? Naturally
And nobody cries,
And nobody cares,
Coz at the end it is just a bad day,
And the bad day will be over.

~ravenraw

Let It Go

Let it go, what you are holding
Nothing permanent, nothing stays
Keep calm, don't hold grudges
Things will happen at their own pace
Stand up, don't be weak
Strength comes when you stand up for yourself
Let it go, of these feelings
Inside you
Feelings are like air, they change
Nothing permanent, nothing stays
Open your arms and hug others
Our presence here is limited
Keep walking, move ahead
What's left has never come back
That's the only way
So let it go

~ravenraw

Goodbye!

Another year has gone by,
Only yesterday we celebrated the new year it
feels like.
We grow and change so much,
but only if we take a look at the passing year.

Again We are making resolutions,
Soon we will be in the run of finding Solutions.
We will be chasing this year's dreams and
demands,
and then Goodbye time will come as a delusion.

How happy and cheerful the world is now,
Everything around us including lighting is just
wow.
We are meeting and greeting each other with
love,
Goodbye month will come when we will wear
gloves.

Life will go on just like these years,
Our memory will fade and it will be a blur.
Soon we will get old and the world will not be
fair,

Goodbye will come again and grey will be our
hair.

~ravenraw

There is no love

How can you live
when there is no love
and everybody thinks
that there is something else
But I know that there is no love
How far they have come
without loving each other
and how can we live when there is no love
We just think it is the same for everyone
while the reality is something else
and everybody is not getting love
So don't you tell me how can you live without
love
I have seen people who don't know love
How can you live
when there is no love
and everybody thinks
there is something else.

~ravenraw

Village Road

I have been on you many times,
but you look more beautiful now,
I think I didn't know what beauty means at that
time,
As I was little and not seen many lives.
You are old to me but look the same,
How many people must have walked?
Still you are unbothered by it,
Many people have left you,
Some might come back to see you,
Lot of whispers you have heard,
Yet you not disclose any of them,
Wildflower blooms around you,
Without water and care,
Still you give them space like a mother,
Now it's time to go to the city,
Will come again in years to see,
Will you wait for me?

~ravenraw

Heartbroken

Heart is broken
Not by a lover
By Life
Is it not fair with everyone?
By choice
Are we all making it wrong?
By Friendship
Why do they get tough over time?
By People
Can't we be a little nice?
My Memories
Do they hurt to make us more alive?

~ravenraw

When You Love SomeOne

When you love someone
You hurt the other one
You can't love everyone
You can't live with all
You got to choose one
The one at a time
When you want something
You have to lose other thing
You can't get everything
There is a sacrifice
We all need to do to live a life
When you love someone
You have to hurt the other one
They can't have you
They must understand
Move on, find else.

~ravenraw

Do You Ever Feel Lonely?

Do you ever feel lonely?
No one else there to understand
You are alone battling your demons
No one there to listen
We all are keeping it to ourselves
Do you ever feel lonely?
Around you many people
Still can't see your fear
In the daylight you walk with a smile
In the night you cry in silence
Do you ever feel lonely?
All the pain you are carrying to where?
Share it with some other
But it will be a burden
So carry it with yourself
Till your last step.

~ravenraw

Home

Home is a feeling,
A place with people,
A Place with Laughter,
A place with Roar,
Feeling can be changed
Over time
So does home,
With the times you live,
In many homes,
One with Family,
One with Friends,
One with Colleagues,
Then you make your own,
Home is a feeling,
You carry with yourself,
From time to time,
and Place to place,
One world to another
Where you stay.
Home is a feeling.

~ravenraw

Rainy Day

Looking outside from my window, waiting to
stop it.
I wanna go outside and play,
I wanna go outside and eat,
I wanna go and dance but only in my head.

It is making a pattern,
Sometimes it's heavy and then slows down a bit,
It's even more beautiful when you are watching
from the mountains,
You can see outside full of greens.

We wanted it and now it's pouring heavily, can't
go out,
Mumma is making tea,
Papa doing the writing,
and I wanna go outside and dance,
But only in my head.

~ravenraw

Life and Problems

19

Life is full of troubles, right?
At every stage,
Still when you were a child.
It's the same for all
Find your own Light.
At every Age
It's not a delight
Have problems
Go do some fight.
At every Phase
with ups and downs
It's around
With No sound.

~ravenraw

Me

I am just me
I don't know how people perceive me
When I meet, they say you are this
I don't know what they wish
I am just me
I don't know how else to be
I wear my style, the one I like
They say it should be like this
The one in style
I am just me
I don't know what they want me to be
Unbound and free, No need for a question,
 Embracing self-expression.
We all are here for different reasons
I can only be me
You can only be you
In a world where beauty shines through.

~ravenraw